50 Warming Drinks for Cold Days

By: Kelly Johnson

Table of Contents

- Hot Chocolate
- Mulled Wine
- Apple Cider
- Chai Latte
- Hot Toddy
- Irish Coffee
- Peppermint Hot Chocolate
- Spiked Eggnog
- Gingerbread Latte
- Cinnamon Spiced Hot Chocolate
- Hot Buttered Rum
- Matcha Latte
- Spiced Pumpkin Latte
- Warm Maple Apple Cider
- Lemon Ginger Tea
- Caramel Latte
- Spiced Red Wine
- Hot Cranberry Punch
- Golden Milk (Turmeric Latte)
- Honey Lemon Tea
- Warm Vanilla Milk
- Hot Ginger Lemonade
- Almond Hot Chocolate
- Eggnog Latte
- Hot Mulled Cranberry Drink
- Hot Mocha
- Choco-Mint Hot Drink
- Hot Lemonade with Thyme
- Cinnamon Tea
- Spiced Chai Hot Chocolate
- Hazelnut Coffee
- Warm Pomegranate Punch
- Hot Coconut Chocolate
- Hot Almond Milk Latte
- Spiked Apple Cider

- Hot Spiced Rum Cider
- Creamy Peppermint Coffee
- Hot Honey Vanilla Latte
- Ginger Honey Tea
- Warm Maple Cinnamon Milk
- Hot Spiked Coffee
- Warm Orange Spice Drink
- Hot Matcha Cocoa
- Warm Cinnamon Honey Tea
- Choco-Banana Drink
- Hot Pear Cinnamon Drink
- Hot Spiced Apricot Drink
- Pomegranate Ginger Tea
- Warm Chai Spiced Wine
- Maple Bourbon Hot Drink

Hot Chocolate

Ingredients:

- 2 cups milk
- 2 tablespoons cocoa powder
- 2 tablespoons sugar
- 1/4 teaspoon vanilla extract
- Pinch of salt
- Whipped cream or marshmallows for topping (optional)

Instructions:

1. In a small saucepan, combine the milk, cocoa powder, sugar, and salt. Heat over medium heat, whisking until the mixture is smooth and hot.
2. Remove from heat and stir in the vanilla extract.
3. Pour into a mug and top with whipped cream or marshmallows, if desired.

Mulled Wine

Ingredients:

- 1 bottle red wine
- 1/4 cup orange juice
- 1/4 cup honey or sugar
- 1 orange, sliced
- 2 cinnamon sticks
- 5-6 whole cloves
- 1 star anise (optional)

Instructions:

1. In a large pot, combine the wine, orange juice, honey, orange slices, cinnamon sticks, cloves, and star anise.
2. Heat over medium-low heat, stirring occasionally, until the mixture is warm (do not boil).
3. Let the wine simmer for 10-15 minutes to allow the flavors to meld.
4. Strain the mulled wine and serve hot in mugs.

Apple Cider

Ingredients:

- 4 cups apple cider
- 2 cinnamon sticks
- 1 orange, sliced
- 5-6 cloves
- 1 tablespoon brown sugar (optional)

Instructions:

1. In a saucepan, combine the apple cider, cinnamon sticks, orange slices, and cloves.
2. Heat over medium heat, stirring occasionally, until the cider is warm.
3. If desired, stir in brown sugar for added sweetness.
4. Simmer for 10-15 minutes, then strain and serve hot.

Chai Latte

Ingredients:

- 1 cup water
- 1 cup milk
- 2 black tea bags
- 2-3 cardamom pods, crushed
- 1 cinnamon stick
- 2-3 whole cloves
- 1/4 inch fresh ginger, sliced
- 1-2 tablespoons honey or sugar

Instructions:

1. In a saucepan, bring water to a boil. Add the tea bags, cardamom pods, cinnamon stick, cloves, ginger, and honey or sugar.
2. Simmer for 5-7 minutes, then remove from heat and add milk.
3. Heat the mixture until warm but not boiling, then strain and serve.

Hot Toddy

Ingredients:

- 1 cup hot water
- 1 ounce whiskey (bourbon, rye, or Scotch)
- 1 tablespoon honey
- 1 tablespoon lemon juice
- 1 cinnamon stick
- Lemon slice for garnish

Instructions:

1. In a mug, combine the hot water, whiskey, honey, and lemon juice.
2. Stir well to dissolve the honey.
3. Add the cinnamon stick and garnish with a lemon slice.
4. Serve hot.

Irish Coffee

Ingredients:

- 1 cup hot coffee
- 1 ounce Irish whiskey
- 1 tablespoon brown sugar
- Whipped cream for topping

Instructions:

1. Brew the coffee and pour it into a mug.
2. Stir in the Irish whiskey and brown sugar until dissolved.
3. Top with whipped cream and serve immediately.

Peppermint Hot Chocolate

Ingredients:

- 2 cups milk
- 2 tablespoons cocoa powder
- 2 tablespoons sugar
- 1/4 teaspoon peppermint extract
- Whipped cream or crushed peppermint for topping

Instructions:

1. In a small saucepan, combine the milk, cocoa powder, and sugar. Heat over medium heat, whisking until smooth and hot.
2. Stir in the peppermint extract and remove from heat.
3. Pour into a mug and top with whipped cream or crushed peppermint.

Spiked Eggnog

Ingredients:

- 1 cup eggnog
- 1 ounce rum or bourbon
- Ground nutmeg for garnish

Instructions:

1. Warm the eggnog in a saucepan over low heat, or microwave it for 30-45 seconds.
2. Stir in the rum or bourbon.
3. Pour into a mug and garnish with a sprinkle of ground nutmeg.

Gingerbread Latte

Ingredients:

- 1 cup brewed espresso or strong coffee
- 1/2 cup milk
- 1 tablespoon gingerbread syrup (or homemade gingerbread spice mix)
- Whipped cream and cinnamon for topping

Instructions:

1. Brew the espresso or coffee and pour into a mug.
2. Heat the milk and gingerbread syrup in a saucepan until warm, then froth if desired.
3. Pour the gingerbread milk mixture over the coffee.
4. Top with whipped cream and a sprinkle of cinnamon.

Cinnamon Spiced Hot Chocolate

Ingredients:

- 2 cups milk
- 2 tablespoons cocoa powder
- 2 tablespoons sugar
- 1/2 teaspoon cinnamon
- Whipped cream or cinnamon sticks for garnish

Instructions:

1. In a small saucepan, combine the milk, cocoa powder, sugar, and cinnamon. Heat over medium heat, whisking until smooth and hot.
2. Remove from heat and pour into a mug.
3. Top with whipped cream or garnish with a cinnamon stick.

Hot Buttered Rum

Ingredients:

- 1 cup hot water
- 2 ounces dark rum
- 1 tablespoon unsalted butter
- 1 tablespoon brown sugar
- 1/4 teaspoon cinnamon
- Pinch of nutmeg
- Whipped cream for topping (optional)

Instructions:

1. In a mug, combine the hot water, rum, butter, brown sugar, cinnamon, and nutmeg.
2. Stir until the butter is melted and the mixture is smooth.
3. Top with whipped cream if desired, and serve hot.

Matcha Latte

Ingredients:

- 1 teaspoon matcha powder
- 1/2 cup hot water
- 1/2 cup steamed milk (or dairy-free milk)
- 1 teaspoon honey or sweetener (optional)

Instructions:

1. Sift the matcha powder into a bowl to remove any clumps.
2. Add the hot water to the matcha powder and whisk vigorously until smooth and frothy.
3. In a separate saucepan, steam the milk until hot but not boiling.
4. Pour the matcha mixture into a mug, then add the steamed milk.
5. Stir in honey or sweetener if desired, and serve.

Spiced Pumpkin Latte

Ingredients:

- 1 cup milk
- 2 tablespoons pumpkin puree
- 1 tablespoon sugar
- 1/2 teaspoon cinnamon
- 1/4 teaspoon nutmeg
- 1/2 teaspoon vanilla extract
- 1 shot espresso or 1/2 cup strong coffee
- Whipped cream for topping

Instructions:

1. In a small saucepan, combine the milk, pumpkin puree, sugar, cinnamon, nutmeg, and vanilla extract. Heat over medium heat, whisking until smooth and warm.
2. Brew the espresso or coffee and pour it into a mug.
3. Pour the pumpkin milk mixture over the coffee and stir.
4. Top with whipped cream and extra cinnamon or nutmeg if desired.

Warm Maple Apple Cider

Ingredients:

- 4 cups apple cider
- 1/4 cup maple syrup
- 1 cinnamon stick
- 1 star anise (optional)
- 1 orange, sliced
- 1/4 teaspoon ground ginger

Instructions:

1. In a saucepan, combine the apple cider, maple syrup, cinnamon stick, star anise, orange slices, and ground ginger.
2. Heat over medium-low heat until warm, but not boiling.
3. Let it simmer for about 10 minutes to infuse the flavors.
4. Strain the cider into mugs and serve warm.

Lemon Ginger Tea

Ingredients:

- 1 cup hot water
- 1-2 slices fresh ginger
- 1 tablespoon lemon juice
- 1 teaspoon honey or sweetener (optional)

Instructions:

1. Boil the water and pour it into a mug.
2. Add the fresh ginger slices to the hot water and let it steep for 5-7 minutes.
3. Remove the ginger slices and stir in the lemon juice and honey if desired.
4. Serve warm.

Caramel Latte

Ingredients:

- 1 shot espresso or 1/2 cup strong coffee
- 1/2 cup steamed milk (or dairy-free milk)
- 2 tablespoons caramel sauce
- Whipped cream for topping

Instructions:

1. Brew the espresso or coffee and pour it into a mug.
2. Steam the milk until hot, but not boiling.
3. Add the caramel sauce to the mug and stir to combine with the coffee.
4. Pour the steamed milk into the mug.
5. Top with whipped cream and a drizzle of caramel sauce.

Spiced Red Wine

Ingredients:

- 1 bottle red wine
- 1 orange, sliced
- 1 cinnamon stick
- 5-6 cloves
- 1/4 cup honey or sugar
- 1 star anise (optional)

Instructions:

1. In a saucepan, combine the red wine, orange slices, cinnamon stick, cloves, honey, and star anise.
2. Heat over medium heat until it is warm (but do not boil).
3. Let it simmer for 10-15 minutes to infuse the flavors.
4. Strain the wine and serve in mugs.

Hot Cranberry Punch

Ingredients:

- 2 cups cranberry juice
- 2 cups apple cider
- 1/4 cup orange juice
- 1 cinnamon stick
- 3-4 whole cloves
- 1 orange, sliced

Instructions:

1. In a saucepan, combine the cranberry juice, apple cider, orange juice, cinnamon stick, cloves, and orange slices.
2. Heat over medium-low heat until warm.
3. Let it simmer for 10-15 minutes to meld the flavors.
4. Strain the punch and serve hot.

Golden Milk (Turmeric Latte)

Ingredients:

- 1 cup milk (or dairy-free milk)
- 1/2 teaspoon turmeric powder
- 1/4 teaspoon cinnamon
- Pinch of black pepper
- 1/2 teaspoon honey or sweetener (optional)
- 1/2 teaspoon vanilla extract (optional)

Instructions:

1. In a saucepan, heat the milk over medium heat.
2. Whisk in the turmeric, cinnamon, black pepper, and honey.
3. Stir until the mixture is smooth and warm, but not boiling.
4. Add vanilla extract if desired, then pour into a mug and serve.

Enjoy these comforting and flavorful drinks!

Honey Lemon Tea

Ingredients:

- 1 cup hot water
- 1 tablespoon honey
- 1 tablespoon fresh lemon juice
- 1-2 lemon slices
- 1/2 teaspoon ginger (optional)

Instructions:

1. Boil the water and pour it into a mug.
2. Stir in the honey and fresh lemon juice until dissolved.
3. Add lemon slices for extra flavor, and ginger if desired.
4. Stir and serve hot.

Warm Vanilla Milk

Ingredients:

- 1 cup milk (or dairy-free milk)
- 1 teaspoon vanilla extract
- 1 tablespoon honey or sugar (optional)
- Pinch of cinnamon (optional)

Instructions:

1. In a small saucepan, heat the milk over medium heat until warm, but not boiling.
2. Stir in the vanilla extract and honey or sugar.
3. Add a pinch of cinnamon for extra flavor (optional).
4. Pour into a mug and serve warm.

Hot Ginger Lemonade

Ingredients:

- 1 cup hot water
- 1 tablespoon fresh lemon juice
- 1 teaspoon grated fresh ginger
- 1 tablespoon honey or sweetener (optional)

Instructions:

1. Boil the water and pour it into a mug.
2. Add the fresh lemon juice and grated ginger.
3. Stir in honey or sweetener if desired.
4. Let it steep for 2-3 minutes, then serve hot.

Almond Hot Chocolate

Ingredients:

- 1 cup almond milk (or dairy-free milk)
- 2 tablespoons cocoa powder
- 1 tablespoon almond butter (optional)
- 1 tablespoon honey or sugar (optional)
- Pinch of cinnamon (optional)

Instructions:

1. In a saucepan, heat the almond milk over medium heat.
2. Whisk in the cocoa powder, almond butter, and sweetener until smooth.
3. Stir until the mixture is hot and well combined.
4. Pour into a mug and sprinkle with cinnamon (optional).

Eggnog Latte

Ingredients:

- 1 shot espresso or 1/2 cup strong coffee
- 1/2 cup eggnog
- 1/2 cup steamed milk (or dairy-free milk)
- Ground nutmeg for garnish

Instructions:

1. Brew the espresso or coffee and pour it into a mug.
2. Heat the eggnog in a saucepan over medium heat until warm, but not boiling.
3. Steam the milk until hot.
4. Pour the eggnog into the coffee and add the steamed milk.
5. Sprinkle with ground nutmeg and serve hot.

Hot Mulled Cranberry Drink

Ingredients:

- 2 cups cranberry juice
- 1 cup apple cider
- 1 cinnamon stick
- 4-5 cloves
- 1 orange, sliced
- 1 tablespoon honey (optional)

Instructions:

1. In a saucepan, combine cranberry juice, apple cider, cinnamon stick, cloves, orange slices, and honey.
2. Heat over medium heat until warm.
3. Simmer for about 10 minutes to infuse the flavors.
4. Strain and serve hot.

Hot Mocha

Ingredients:

- 1 shot espresso or 1/2 cup strong coffee
- 1/2 cup milk (or dairy-free milk)
- 2 tablespoons cocoa powder
- 1 tablespoon sugar or sweetener (optional)
- Whipped cream (optional)

Instructions:

1. Brew the espresso or coffee and pour it into a mug.
2. In a saucepan, heat the milk and whisk in the cocoa powder and sugar until smooth.
3. Pour the chocolate milk mixture into the coffee and stir.
4. Top with whipped cream (optional) and serve hot.

Choco-Mint Hot Drink

Ingredients:

- 1 cup milk (or dairy-free milk)
- 2 tablespoons cocoa powder
- 1/4 teaspoon peppermint extract
- 1 tablespoon sugar or sweetener (optional)
- Whipped cream (optional)
- Crushed mint candies (optional)

Instructions:

1. Heat the milk in a saucepan over medium heat.
2. Whisk in the cocoa powder, peppermint extract, and sweetener.
3. Stir until smooth and hot.
4. Pour into a mug, and top with whipped cream and crushed mint candies if desired.

Hot Lemonade with Thyme

Ingredients:

- 1 cup hot water
- 1 tablespoon fresh lemon juice
- 1 teaspoon fresh thyme (or 1/2 teaspoon dried thyme)
- 1 tablespoon honey or sweetener (optional)

Instructions:

1. Boil the water and pour it into a mug.
2. Add the lemon juice and fresh thyme.
3. Stir in honey or sweetener if desired.
4. Let it steep for 2-3 minutes, then remove the thyme.
5. Serve hot.

Cinnamon Tea

Ingredients:

- 1 cup hot water
- 1 cinnamon stick
- 1 teaspoon honey or sweetener (optional)
- 1 tablespoon fresh lemon juice (optional)

Instructions:

1. Boil the water and pour it into a mug.
2. Add the cinnamon stick and let it steep for about 5 minutes.
3. Stir in honey or sweetener, and lemon juice if desired.
4. Remove the cinnamon stick, then serve hot.

Spiced Chai Hot Chocolate

Ingredients:

- 1 cup milk (or dairy-free milk)
- 2 tablespoons cocoa powder
- 1 chai tea bag or 1 tablespoon loose chai tea
- 1 tablespoon honey or sugar (optional)
- 1/4 teaspoon cinnamon
- Pinch of cloves (optional)

Instructions:

1. Heat the milk in a saucepan over medium heat.
2. Steep the chai tea bag (or loose tea) in the milk for 3-5 minutes.
3. Whisk in the cocoa powder, cinnamon, and sweetener until smooth.
4. Remove the tea bag, pour into a mug, and serve hot.

Hazelnut Coffee

Ingredients:

- 1 cup brewed coffee
- 1 tablespoon hazelnut syrup or hazelnut extract
- 1/4 cup milk (or dairy-free milk)
- Whipped cream (optional)
- Crushed hazelnuts for garnish (optional)

Instructions:

1. Brew your coffee and pour it into a mug.
2. Stir in the hazelnut syrup or extract.
3. Heat the milk and froth it if desired.
4. Pour the frothed milk into the coffee, top with whipped cream, and garnish with crushed hazelnuts.

Warm Pomegranate Punch

Ingredients:

- 2 cups pomegranate juice
- 1 cup apple cider
- 1 cinnamon stick
- 4-5 whole cloves
- 1 orange, sliced
- 1 tablespoon honey (optional)

Instructions:

1. Combine the pomegranate juice, apple cider, cinnamon stick, cloves, and orange slices in a saucepan.
2. Heat over medium heat until warm, but not boiling.
3. Stir in honey for extra sweetness (optional).
4. Remove the spices and serve hot.

Hot Coconut Chocolate

Ingredients:

- 1 cup coconut milk
- 2 tablespoons cocoa powder
- 1 tablespoon honey or sugar (optional)
- 1/4 teaspoon vanilla extract
- Shredded coconut for garnish (optional)

Instructions:

1. Heat the coconut milk in a saucepan over medium heat.
2. Whisk in the cocoa powder, sweetener, and vanilla extract until smooth.
3. Once hot, pour into a mug, and garnish with shredded coconut if desired.

Hot Almond Milk Latte

Ingredients:

- 1 shot espresso or 1/2 cup strong coffee
- 1/2 cup almond milk
- 1/2 tablespoon maple syrup or sweetener (optional)
- Ground cinnamon for garnish (optional)

Instructions:

1. Brew the espresso or coffee and pour it into a mug.
2. Heat the almond milk over medium heat, then froth it.
3. Pour the frothed almond milk into the coffee and stir in the maple syrup or sweetener.
4. Garnish with a sprinkle of ground cinnamon (optional) and serve hot.

Spiked Apple Cider

Ingredients:

- 2 cups apple cider
- 1 cinnamon stick
- 1 orange, sliced
- 1 tablespoon honey or sugar (optional)
- 1 ounce rum or bourbon (optional)

Instructions:

1. Heat the apple cider with the cinnamon stick and orange slices in a saucepan.
2. Simmer for 10-15 minutes to infuse the flavors.
3. Stir in honey or sweetener if desired.
4. Remove the cinnamon stick, then pour into a mug.
5. Add rum or bourbon for a spiked version (optional), and serve hot.

Hot Spiced Rum Cider

Ingredients:

- 2 cups apple cider
- 1 cinnamon stick
- 1/2 teaspoon ground nutmeg
- 1/2 teaspoon ground cloves
- 1 ounce dark rum
- Orange slices for garnish

Instructions:

1. In a saucepan, heat the apple cider with the cinnamon stick, nutmeg, and cloves over medium heat.
2. Once hot, remove from heat and stir in the dark rum.
3. Pour into a mug, garnish with orange slices, and serve hot.

Creamy Peppermint Coffee

Ingredients:

- 1 cup brewed coffee
- 1/4 cup heavy cream or dairy-free cream
- 1 tablespoon peppermint syrup or 1/2 teaspoon peppermint extract
- Whipped cream for topping (optional)
- Crushed candy canes for garnish (optional)

Instructions:

1. Brew the coffee and pour it into a mug.
2. Heat the heavy cream in a saucepan until warm, then stir in the peppermint syrup or extract.
3. Pour the creamy mixture into the coffee and stir well.
4. Top with whipped cream and garnish with crushed candy canes if desired.

Hot Honey Vanilla Latte

Ingredients:

- 1 shot espresso or 1/2 cup strong coffee
- 1/2 cup milk (or dairy-free milk)
- 1 tablespoon honey
- 1/2 teaspoon vanilla extract
- Ground cinnamon for garnish (optional)

Instructions:

1. Brew the espresso or strong coffee and pour it into a mug.
2. Heat the milk in a saucepan over medium heat and froth it.
3. Stir in the honey and vanilla extract into the coffee.
4. Pour the frothed milk into the coffee, top with ground cinnamon (optional), and serve hot.

Ginger Honey Tea

Ingredients:

- 1 cup hot water
- 1-2 teaspoons fresh ginger, grated
- 1 tablespoon honey
- 1/2 teaspoon lemon juice (optional)

Instructions:

1. Boil the water and pour it into a mug.
2. Add the grated ginger and let it steep for 5-7 minutes.
3. Strain out the ginger, then stir in honey and lemon juice (if desired).
4. Serve hot and enjoy.

Warm Maple Cinnamon Milk

Ingredients:

- 1 cup milk (or dairy-free milk)
- 1 tablespoon maple syrup
- 1/4 teaspoon cinnamon
- Pinch of nutmeg (optional)

Instructions:

1. Heat the milk in a saucepan over medium heat until warm.
2. Stir in the maple syrup and cinnamon.
3. Add a pinch of nutmeg for extra warmth (optional).
4. Pour into a mug and serve hot.

Hot Spiked Coffee

Ingredients:

- 1 cup brewed coffee
- 1 ounce whiskey or bourbon
- 1 tablespoon brown sugar
- Whipped cream for topping (optional)

Instructions:

1. Brew your coffee and pour it into a mug.
2. Stir in the whiskey or bourbon and brown sugar until dissolved.
3. Top with whipped cream for an extra indulgence (optional).
4. Serve hot and enjoy.

Warm Orange Spice Drink

Ingredients:

- 1 cup orange juice
- 1/2 cup water
- 1 cinnamon stick
- 2-3 whole cloves
- 1 tablespoon honey (optional)

Instructions:

1. In a saucepan, combine the orange juice, water, cinnamon stick, and cloves.
2. Heat over medium heat, allowing the spices to infuse for about 5-7 minutes.
3. Stir in honey if desired, and strain out the spices.
4. Pour into a mug and serve hot.

Hot Matcha Cocoa

Ingredients:

- 1 cup milk (or dairy-free milk)
- 1 tablespoon matcha powder
- 1 tablespoon cocoa powder
- 1 tablespoon honey or sweetener (optional)
- 1/2 teaspoon vanilla extract (optional)

Instructions:

1. Heat the milk in a saucepan over medium heat until warm.
2. In a small bowl, whisk together the matcha powder and cocoa powder.
3. Add the powders to the milk, and stir in honey and vanilla (optional).
4. Once smooth, pour into a mug and serve hot.

Warm Cinnamon Honey Tea

Ingredients:

- 1 cup hot water
- 1 cinnamon stick
- 1 tablespoon honey
- 1-2 slices fresh ginger (optional)

Instructions:

1. Boil the water and pour it into a mug.
2. Add the cinnamon stick and ginger slices (if using) to the hot water.
3. Let it steep for 5-7 minutes.
4. Stir in honey and serve hot.

Choco-Banana Drink

Ingredients:

- 1 cup milk (or dairy-free milk)
- 1/2 ripe banana
- 2 tablespoons cocoa powder
- 1 tablespoon honey or sweetener (optional)
- 1/4 teaspoon vanilla extract (optional)

Instructions:

1. Blend the banana, cocoa powder, and milk until smooth.
2. Heat the mixture in a saucepan over medium heat until warm.
3. Stir in honey and vanilla extract if desired.
4. Pour into a mug and serve hot.

Hot Pear Cinnamon Drink

Ingredients:

- 1 cup pear juice
- 1/2 cup water
- 1 cinnamon stick
- 1 tablespoon honey (optional)
- 1-2 slices of fresh ginger (optional)

Instructions:

1. In a saucepan, combine the pear juice, water, and cinnamon stick.
2. Heat over medium heat and let it simmer for 5-7 minutes to infuse the cinnamon flavor.
3. Stir in honey if desired and add the fresh ginger slices for extra warmth.
4. Remove the cinnamon stick and strain out the ginger.
5. Pour into a mug and serve hot.

Hot Spiced Apricot Drink

Ingredients:

- 1 cup apricot nectar
- 1/2 cup water
- 1/4 teaspoon ground cinnamon
- 1/4 teaspoon ground ginger
- 1 tablespoon honey (optional)

Instructions:

1. In a saucepan, combine the apricot nectar, water, ground cinnamon, and ground ginger.
2. Heat over medium heat, stirring occasionally, until warm.
3. Stir in honey if desired for sweetness.
4. Pour into a mug and serve hot.

Pomegranate Ginger Tea

Ingredients:

- 1 cup hot water
- 1 tablespoon pomegranate juice
- 1-2 slices fresh ginger
- 1 tablespoon honey (optional)
- 1/2 teaspoon lemon juice (optional)

Instructions:

1. Boil the water and pour it into a mug.
2. Add the pomegranate juice and fresh ginger slices to the hot water.
3. Let it steep for 5-7 minutes to infuse the ginger flavor.
4. Stir in honey and lemon juice if desired.
5. Strain the ginger and serve hot.

Warm Chai Spiced Wine

Ingredients:

- 1 cup red wine
- 1/2 cup water
- 1 cinnamon stick
- 2-3 whole cloves
- 2-3 cardamom pods (lightly crushed)
- 1-2 tablespoons honey or sugar (optional)

Instructions:

1. In a saucepan, combine the red wine, water, cinnamon stick, cloves, and cardamom pods.
2. Heat over medium heat until warm, but do not let it boil.
3. Stir in honey or sugar if desired.
4. Simmer for about 5-7 minutes to allow the spices to infuse.
5. Strain and pour into a mug, serving warm.

Maple Bourbon Hot Drink

Ingredients:

- 1 cup hot water
- 1 ounce bourbon
- 1 tablespoon maple syrup
- 1/4 teaspoon ground cinnamon
- 1/4 teaspoon ground nutmeg
- Whipped cream (optional)

Instructions:

1. Boil the water and pour it into a mug.
2. Stir in the bourbon, maple syrup, ground cinnamon, and ground nutmeg.
3. Mix well until the syrup is dissolved.
4. Top with whipped cream for extra richness (optional).
5. Serve hot and enjoy!

www.ingramcontent.com/pod-product-compliance
Lightning Source LLC
LaVergne TN
LVHW061957070526
838199LV00060B/4166